PEOP|

C000064753

I love the book - it is profoun
Anamika imparts as a teacher an

—————

"Curious Case of Benjamin Button"

Anamika's message could not arrive at a better time. Perhaps if I keep
this book really close, I will learn to live by its wisdom.
—Barnet Bain, Producer
"What Dreams May Come" and
"The Celestine Prophecy"

and…takes you out of the realm of the mind so you can embody the
unique brilliance of these truths. What an amazing experience!
—Jennifer Goodrich, Singer/Songwriter

This book is about a metamorphosis of unimaginable proportions. I
could feel the energy all the way through!
—Michael Goodrich, Vocal Coach

This book is uniquely experiential and calls forth one's greater sense
of self.
—Barbara Hamilton, International Consultant

When we say "but" or "or," we put a stop in place. and… opens us
up boundless possibility. It's not a one-time read; something new is
always revealed!
—Irene Mink, Stylist

Every sentence is a potent life-changing truth.
—Leerone, Artist

Also by Anamika

French Lessons in Love...and some lessons in language too

Love in Fur Coats: Gifts from my Animal Companions

Loving Now

and...

ANAMIKA

Copyright ©2014 by Anamika

Special contributions: Stephan Choiniere

Edited by: Carrie Zivetz, Laurel Airica, Irene Mink

Special thanks to: Robin Swicord, Tom Schulman, Barnet Bain, Steve Parrish, Xavier Chesneau, Greg Winters, Julianna and Mac Parker, Michael and Jennifer Goodrich, Katerina Getchell

Cover photos and front cover design by Norman Seeff
Back cover by Stephan Choiniere

Formatted by Karen Richardson

ISBN: 978-0-9886879-6-7

More information at www.anamika.com

and... / Anamika.

CONTENTS

this little book

This little book is about big change.

We're in a time as never before. We are evolving into ways of being that are completely different from what we have known, what we've experienced and who we've been. This transition into a more expansive and inclusive consciousness will have a far greater impact on us all than the discovery that the Earth is round. It accounts for the exponential quickening and intensity of this extraordinary time in our history.

Each era is a dream that dies as a new one is being birthed. The recent chaos, violence and breakdown of the old order are indicative of having reached the extremes of our current way of being. This collapse of the old ways is occurring within each of us and on a national and global level.

For a way of being, an operating system or paradigm, to collapse, it has to reach its edges and consume itself. We are at those edges and see that we can't continue to live the way we have. This awareness precipitates change not only within us, but also in how we deal with one another and the planet as a whole.

We are changing.
Our world is changing.

Our sense of reality is changing, as is our sense of who we are individually and together.

In this process, we are feeling the turbulence inherent in change, which calls for an expansion of our consciousness. It calls us deeper into the mystery of the unknown to discover new possibilities and an interconnected and generous love.

Despite the enormous suffering that still exists in our world, I feel that we've already crossed a line into birthing a brighter future. Becoming more acutely aware of our darkness is part of this forward movement. As we expand beyond our current limitations, we're learning what it means to be human in more caring and inclusive ways.

In this journey together, I invite you to read this book not only with your mind, but to feel the energy of the words and ideas in your heart, your body, your emotions, and your sensations. I invite you to discover who you are beyond who you currently think you are. In openness, something new emerges and we evolve.

As you read, please allow familiar words to take on new meaning. For example, I've used the everyday word "and" in a different way. Ordinarily, we use the word "and" when we want to link two things together. When we experience this and then that, it adds more, which changes the quantity of something. But it doesn't change the quality or nature of the things into becoming something else.

This happens through a different process than simple addition. Something fundamentally changes when we experience two or more things simultaneously. In this instance, a brand new experience occurs. We come to know more of what was unknown, more of who we are.

My use of "*and..*" connotes both the process of inclusivity and the new states of being that continuously arise as a result of it. You can think of it as "andness," the wondrous process of unfolding and becoming that is the nature of creation itself.

and.. allows everything to be there without judgment. In its resonances we embrace paradox, seemingly opposite or contradictory things simultaneously, and they create something new.

and.. is where evolution is inviting us to go.

In its metamorphosis, a caterpillar is transformed into a whole new being following a total dissolution of its previous form. A butterfly is not a caterpillar with wings. We, too, are becoming something new, something greater than we were, far beyond who we've been, beyond what we've dreamed, and beyond our ability to imagine. We are recreating ourselves, our world, and our reality as we shed what has been and grow into more of who we are.

We are powerful creators who create reality daily, but usually without awareness of doing so. As we learn to create consciously, our power to create is limitless from a continuous, flexible, generative flow. In fact, we are that flow itself.

To create a new world, we slip into the ineffable mystery of the flow where words, ideas, thoughts and definitions can't go. There, we touch indefinable depths, richness and expansiveness. In partnering these realms, we and all that exists become more.

As a natural expression of our new resonances, we create a more loving world. In becoming an artist of life itself, we birth new creation in which we create and are created at the same time.

where we are

In any era, the strongest matrix of ideas becomes a paradigm. It is a pattern through which what we call reality manifests. This pattern takes on a life of its own becomes an operating system. It is the "box" whose edges constrain our thinking.

There have been different paradigms in operation on our planet – different stories that we have called reality. We've had matriarchies based on instinct, deriving power from nature, dependence and giving. We've had patriarchies based on intellect, independence, taking, and power over nature as well as over other people. The paradigm we are outgrowing is some blend of what has gone before.

At some point, all paradigms stop working and collapse. That's where we are right now. Many people are sensing possibilities beyond the current world consensus, even though the majority still live within in it. We've been this way for so long that many don't see its limitations or believe there are other options. Yet, we're creating a positive future that's never existed before within ourselves and together.

The principles of the old paradigm became rigid ideologies, dogmas and rules to follow in order to survive. They are the antithesis of creativity and creation. When inside its operating system, which we call "reality," we believe that we must apply its rules to get our needs met. When adhering to rules, we can't imagine venturing into uncharted territory where there aren't any rules and we can trust the flow of Love to guide us.

When paradigms change, so does reality. To evolve beyond our current system so that we can create anew, it's vital to become aware of its principles and rules.

rules

We have authentic needs for love, safety, belonging, and so on. But how do these needs get met? The old operating system dictates that we must get our needs met from "out there." We're supposed to figure out how to get the resources, which we believe are limited, in order to meet our needs. We are taught that these resources are *not* inherent, limitless and within us right now as resonances which precipitate effortlessly into physical form. We believe these resonances are not who we already are and therefore it takes effort to get our needs to survive met. We believe our needs get met with some degree of difficulty by external things to acquire, consume and possess. Since we believe it's hard to survive, we believe if we figure out how to follow the rules, we'll succeed in getting our needs met.

The prevailing rules of the old reality:

> It's up to me to get my needs met.
> It's up to me to figure out how.

I must work hard to get my needs met.

Good things must be earned.

My needs get met from the outside.

I must be in control to make it happen.

I must take care of myself all by myself.

Never be dependent, weak, or vulnerable.

Never lose control.

If I lose control I'll be powerless to get my
needs met.

I must get it right and do it right.

There's only so much pie to go around
because resources are limited.

I don't have what I need.

I don't have access to infinite inner resource.

I have to fight for what I want.

Since all of my needs are not met, I must be
doing something wrong.

I must be fundamentally flawed.

I must please some authority out there
(parents, teachers, employer, society, God)
to earn the resource.

There's an authority out there whose
judgment and punishment I must avoid
or endure.

I must follow the rules perfectly.

My value is measured by how I compare
with others.

I have to compete against others to survive.

Only the one top dog gets the meat.

To make sure to be the one to survive, I must
be quick to judge, criticize, punish and kill.

The world is out there, separate from me,
and it's a scary place.

It's me against the world.

If things were different, then I'd get my
needs met.

Don't dream, don't imagine.

Don't trust instincts or intuition, only logic.

I must be fiercely independent, separate and
autonomous.

I must have power over and against nature
and people so that I can win.

Power comes from domination and
intimidation.

Nature and animals exist to serve us.

Take from others to meet your needs before
you're taken.

Kill or be killed.

Others and nature are the enemy.

I should be able to do whatever I want
whenever I want.

Status is measured by power over and
against, and brute strength.

Life is about suffering and enduring.

I am utterly alone.

I don't belong.

I'm not enough.

I don't have enough.

Quantity is valued over quality.

I am alienated and disconnected.

Life happens to me.

Life is not the way I want it to be.

I am a victim, not a powerful creator.

The ego "I" is the all-powerful creator.

I'm not inherently one with all of creation.

I am not part of a loving, evolving whole.

I don't have access to all of existence.

I don't create my own experience.

I don't create my reality, it happens to me.

The old way says that in following these rules, we will earn the love, safety, abundance we need in order to survive. We have believed that to be true. Yet no matter what we attain, achieve, possess, acquire, or accumulate, we still feel scared, alone and empty in some way. This way of being hasn't succeeded in meeting our real needs.

We are powerful creators, yet we say we're not. We have infinite resources within us, yet we say that we don't. We have authentic needs that we say we can't meet effortlessly from within.

Instead, we're taught that being in control and taking power over and against is how we master life and meet our needs. As such, we do everything and anything to dominate and intimidate. Yet, holding onto control and following these rules actually keeps us separate and prevents us from meeting our needs.

There's nothing wrong with this system or our participation in it. In fact, it's been a valuable part of our human journey as a stage of development. However, having arrived at the point of realizing that this way is not working and creates suffering, we're ready to grow.

When we're struggling and suffering, we can't feel our heart. We live in an internal wilderness in which we are hardwired to operate out of fear and do whatever it takes to survive.

survival

In the wilderness, survival of the fittest is natural. The law is to kill or be killed.

Even though we're no longer living in the wilderness, we continue to behave as if we are from a hardwired belief that our survival is at stake. We feel threatened emotionally, economically, socially and physically.

I'm not safe.
There's not enough.
It's up to me to protect and defend myself and others.
I have to be on red alert, ready for fight or flight.

We reflexively default to our fight or flight mechanism. When we believe that there are not enough resources to survive, we are willing to engage in ruthless competition, domination, victimization, violence, and war. This pits us against each other in a fight to acquire and control resources.

We genuinely believe this strategy is ensuring our safety. Yet, we never feel truly safe. In fact, we don't feel much at all, even though we think we are feeling. We have to numb our feelings to compete against and kill each other. Numbing ourselves emotionally and physically, by whatever means we do it, causes terrible suffering for ourselves and those around us.

Survival is one of the most pervasive and convincing of human stories and it doesn't allow us to live peaceably and thrive. It causes immeasurable suffering.

right

To survive, we have to make sure to be the one to get it right. Otherwise we are not the one who survives.

The harder we try to get it right, the more pain we cause.

We think:
    I know best.
    I know how it should be and what's right.
    I have to have it my way.
    I can bend life to my will.

Then:
    I'll have power.
    I'll be good enough to be rewarded.
    I'll get my needs met.
    I'll be special.
    I'll be happy.

Therefore:
    I need to be right.
    I must do it right.

I work hard to be right.
I must be better than you.
I can't make mistakes.
I must be perfect.
By being right, I can get rid of what's wrong.
I must be especially and righteously good,
    not bad.
If I can't be perfectly good, I pretend I don't
    care and rebel, so I can be especially and
    righteously bad.
Who I am just as me is not ok.

But, in fact:
Needing to be right makes me self-righteous.
Needing to be right is about keeping score.
It's about competition and comparison.
It's about judgment and 'make wrong.'
It's about defending my rules.
It keeps me limited to a right answer, a right
    way, and a right "One."
Trying to be right creates false hope of
    success.
It limits possibilities.
It doesn't make me safe.
It doesn't make me happy.

Because:

> If I'm right I'm good but If I'm wrong I'm
>   bad.
> If I'm right then you're wrong.
> If I'm right, I'm better than you.
> If I'm wrong then you're right.
> If I'm wrong, I'm worse than you.
> It's either/or, you or me.
> I think that either/or is win or lose.
> But it's really lose/lose.

Lose/lose imprisons our hearts.

judgment

We suffer terribly when we feel separate from our heart and our dignity of being.

We separate from our love by comparing ourselves, and each other, to some false standard of perfection. We think that we're supposed to be other than who or where we are. When we judge, we feel disconnected from our limitless internal resource, lightness and freedom.

In this comparison, we either consider ourselves inferior or superior. Judgments can be positive or negative. In either case, we're filled with false pride or false humility, arrogance, disdain, disgust, resistance, hatred and violence towards ourselves, each other, and being human itself.

In the darkness of separation from our inner Source, which we create through judgment of ourselves and others, we may conclude that there must be something wrong with us or with everyone else. We must be fundamentally flawed or out of sync with the times and the people around us. It seems completely hopeless to do anything about it, and we'd just as soon die.

Certain "preferences," or things we think we want are actually judgments because they come from the intellect and not from our heart. When we're willing to surrender what we think we want and allow for what's so in the moment, there's freedom in which we can sense our true heart's desires.

As much as we crave this heart connection, we instinctively protect against further hurt. From years of becoming distant, unfeeling and defended, we may have even lost sight that it's possible to open, or we have lost access as to how to allow it. In its extreme form, we act out violence on ourselves, or others, saying that if I could just get rid of myself, or you, I'd be ok. I'm the problem, or you're the problem.

Judgment is a prison. It's closed at both ends and freezes everything in place. It eliminates flexibility and possibility. There's no movement, flow or growth. Discernment, by contrast, is open, as it includes compassion. Through discernment we make choices without the judgment that says things are 'bad' or 'wrong.'

According to many sources, we fell from grace. Yet, Grace is the natural flow of our being when we're standing in Love. But we didn't just "fall from grace." It happens each moment when we judge instead of love. Then, we spend our lives trying to prove our worth and be in control to compensate for the lack of love.

What if our interpretation of "falling from grace" is that something went wrong? We didn't fall from some idealized state to which we're trying to return. What if we didn't say that contractions are wrong? We can progress by seeing what doesn't work. When we don't judge ourselves as "bad" we evolve. Through discernment, forgiveness and compassion, we can discover the gems that are in everything. As such, we expand even beyond where we were before.

control

It's vital that our real needs be met. But how we go about that fulfillment makes all the difference between grace and suffering.

When our needs are not met, we feel threatened. It seems urgent, like life or death. We go to any lengths to assure our needs are met and to defend ourselves against imagined future hurts.

However, when our needs are not met, it isn't because we have failed to attain or obtain something. We are taught that the source of what we need comes from outside of us and that we don't have access within to the fullness we are seeking. We think there is an inherent lack or something missing within us. For example: if I had enough money, or my dream career, or if I looked just right, or married the perfect "One" all of my needs would be met. Then I would finally be who I want to be, and feel the way I want to feel. Then my life would work.

From this perspective, what we are really saying is that we are separate from the limitless Love that is already within us. When we don't believe it's there, we need someone to give it to us, try to get it ourselves, or try to be beyond need. For example, when we believe we are separate from limitless abundance, we think money will make us safe.

When we begin with the premise that we are lacking and must fill the hole, we try to exert control to do that. Our underlying intention, when we exercise control, is to meet our needs. But since we believe that what we need is lacking within us, there's a survival threat involved. To try to ensure our survival, we resort to manipulating, dominating, possessing, consuming, restraining, forcing, defending, judging, pushing, pulling, driving, punishing, preventing, perfecting and so on. We do this to others as well as to ourselves.

I must DO something to get my needs met RIGHT NOW.
I must get it, or get you to give it to me.

From a perspective of inner lack, we are powerless and imagine that there's an outside authority with the power to hurt or help, grant or deny.

This imagined authority could be parents, teachers, employers, government, religion, drugs, food, God/Goddess, angels, The One, or anything else to which we look to be fulfilled.

We expend an enormous amount of energy trying to get it "right" and be good enough to earn reward and avoid punishment. Yet, underneath it all, it's never quite right enough. Something is still missing.

> If there weren't something missing,
>   everything would be perfect.
> But since it's not perfect, that proves there's
>   something wrong.
> It's up to me to fix it.
> Since I can never fix everything, or be
>   perfect enough, there must be something
>   wrong with me, or with the world.
> It must be my fault, or… it must be their fault.
> I have to do something to control myself, my
>   life, and everyone else.

We try to control everything, even life and death. We have the illusion that when we finally get it "right," and finally become so powerful, perfect, and in control, we will no longer have anything to fear.

Though we are convinced that exerting control will meet our needs, it actually doesn't. Not only is the effort of the exertion depleting, attempting to control outcome doesn't really work and never will.

In fact, we end up giving away our true power and still don't feel deeply safe, cherished, peaceful, and free. While control may accomplish things, fundamental needs are still yearning to be met underneath it all.

This is because our fundamental needs are feeling states, not things.

When we attempt to access a feeling state through exerting control, it doesn't work. We just think it will. Like an addict seeking the next "fix," we grasp at more and more control, thinking this time we will succeed in meeting our fundamental needs. We try harder and harder, exerting more and more control.

The more we exert control, the less we truly feel. The less we feel, the more we retreat into our heads and make up stories, explanations and justifications for our circumstances. We become anxious and depressed.

Taking charge is different than being in control. Taking charge is choosing the state of being we're standing in, not controlling something outside of ourselves. Taking charge is not forcing an action. We take charge of our inner frequency and the external doing follows naturally from our inner resonant state of being.

Even when people start to open up to being in charge in an empowering way, they may still want to hold onto control in case they need it some day. The belief that control will work is deeply ingrained.

stories

Imagine this: You are standing on a street corner and a bus comes barreling over the curb directly at you. Your survival would be threatened, and you'd naturally go into a fight or flight reflex to save your life.

But—if you are standing on a street corner waiting for the light to change, and you occupy your mind with "imagining" a bus barreling over the curb… that's storytelling.

This kind of storytelling is a repetitive mental loop that creates drama. It distances us from actually experiencing the present. It is based on the belief that our emotional and physical survival is at stake. This kind of storytelling is a mental activity, not an authentically feeling one.

We make up positive and negative stories. We tell scary stories, and then try to replace them with comforting ones. We "think positive" in an attempt to protect, justify, fix or save. Or we make up even scarier stories, preferring negativity.

Stories, whether positive or negative, are the result of an unwillingness to actually feel. What we call "feelings" when we are in a story is the drama that results from not feeling. In drama, there is no real movement of energy.

> We are great storytellers.
> We tell stories day and night.
> We tell them with conviction.
> We tell them over and over again.
> Through repetition we reinforce our stories.
> We become more convinced that they're real.
> We become more and more attached to our stories.
> We cease to question their content as we get drawn into their drama.
> We write the script, direct the play and act out he parts.
> We play victim, martyr, persecutor, judge, objector, protector, hero, rescuer, and savior.
> We feel these roles as reality.
> We engage others in our drama.
> We see how our audience reacts.

We enact the same drama again and again.
We believe it's happening to us.
We believe we have no ability to choose
    differently.

Suffering comes from the stories we make up and then believe. Some of our most widely agreed upon stories are:

There's something wrong with me.
I need to be better than I am.
I should be perfect.

I'm not enough.
I'm too much.
I am not loved or lovable.
I am not of value.
I am not safe and secure.
I don't belong.
I don't have what I need within me.
I have to get what I need outside of me.
I am worse than.
I am better than.
I am inferior.
I am superior.

If I'm good enough, someone else will take
    care of me.
If I'm good enough, I won't need anyone else.
I can take care of myself.
If I'm good enough, I'll be approved of.
If I'm not good enough, I'll be rejected,
    abandoned, and abused.

I am alone.
I am separate.
I don't belong.

The outside world is the "real" world.
Life happens to me.
I need to be in control.
I have no control.
It's all up to me.

I want it my way.
I want what I want when I want it, and I
    want it now.
I can never have what I want
I want it different than it is.

I have to find the perfect "One."
I have to be the perfect "One."

I need to do something to survive.

We tell stories in which we are disconnected and separate.

We also tell stories in which we imagine ourselves abundant and connected. In telling both kinds of stories, positive or negative, we actually render ourselves powerless.

When we are telling stories, we are not in the present. We are referencing from the past and projecting into the future. Rather than just feeling what's so in the moment, we're trying to be in control in an attempt to meet our needs. But it doesn't work.

When we're telling stories, it stops the flow of authentic feeling. We try to escape feeling by becoming free of emotion, instead of free to feel emotion.

> True emotion flows through the heart.
> The heart doesn't tell stories.
> It feels… it doesn't control.
>
> Not feeling causes suffering.

suffering

It seems that the source of suffering comes from our circumstances.

But it doesn't.

Suffering comes from wanting ourselves or our circumstances to be different than they are right now. Suffering comes from saying 'no' to what is, as if who I am and where I am in this moment are not ok. In judging, which is rejecting who and where we are, we push away from feeling. When we don't feel our joy and our pain, we can't experience that we are whole, loveable and wonderful, no matter what we think about what we've done or what is happening right now.

When we separate from our natural feelings, which include a sense of infinite vastness, we experience emptiness or lack, as if something is missing. Then we can't feel we are boundless. We don't experience that we're already abundant, beautiful, and wise just as we are. We don't know that what we really need, and wish to feel, is accessible right now. Hence, we can't choose to align with it.

When we don't feel whole, we conjure up a mental agenda of what we think we need, want and should be. These dreams, wishes, and visions are actually ego's demands, not heart's desires. Trying to implement these limited ideas stops the movement of our energy. When we can't feel the flow of our infinite energy, we suffer. We feel stuck, believing we're never enough and always in need of improvement. Then we become:

frustrated, impatient
anxious, desperate, afraid
stressed, strained
clenched, tense
depleted, exhausted
discouraged, depressed

sick, in pain
humiliated, blaming, shaming
outraged, in-raged
hostile, rejecting, rebellious
vengeful, vindictive
self-pitying, punishing
resentful.

We give up, run away,
submit, escape, check out,
break down,
don't care,
apathetic in despair,
want to die.

We pick ourselves up.
Try harder.
Fight harder.

Work longer, go faster, do more.
Spike adrenaline.
Push, dominate, demand.
Consume, possess.

It's not working.

Complain, plead, submit.
Powerless and hopeless.
Utterly separate, completely alone.
Insular, isolated.
Collapsed.
Numb.
Still not working.
Crisis occurs.

This is the cycle of suffering.

awakening

We wish to be free of bondage and the suffering it causes. We yearn for something beyond the ordinary.

Humanity is now yearning for the experience of knowing ourselves as one world and as part of a greater whole. It seems that that over the past 100,000 years or so we have been actively developing our ability to consciously connect in wholeness.

We long to actually feel ourselves as one with All-That-Is as a tangible experience. We can sense that who we are is greater than what we have thought of as our ordinary selves. We are now at a turning point in human history with the capacity for countless people to fulfill that realization instead of destroying ourselves.

As we make our transition through this unprecedented time, we are experiencing the birthing pains and great changes of a new era. We are successfully expanding beyond our current stage of development. This is a process beyond simply growing, which only entails more volume. Actual awakening is expanding and deepening in all directions simultaneously. Expanding into this way in this new cycle is a most challenging, yet exhilarating transformation that I believe will peak around 2050 for humanity as a whole.

As we see through the veils of what we thought was reality, we're birthing a much brighter future. This quantum leap in human consciousness has never before occurred: not on this planet, not in all creation, and not in all eternity.

Who we are in reality is so much more expansive than we've ever known or can ever understand. Who we really are extends far beyond our body, our personality, our life and our world. Our limitless nature is active, dynamic and ever changing.

We've tried to know ourselves by answering the age-old question, "Who am I?" We can describe our appearance, likes and dislikes, personality traits, skills and talents, as well as what we do. But, we cannot describe who we are, because that is not something we can intellectually understand.

The uncharted territory of our own being is something the rational mind alone can never comprehend, but it can be deeply felt and experienced. While the mind wants to understand, explain and define, the heart says, "Go experience, because intellectual understanding alone isn't adequate to describe the poetry of real aliveness."

Experiencing is different than explaining. Understanding grows through experiencing. Deep understanding includes intellectual, emotional, visceral, and revelatory perceptions and more. As it emerges from the depths of our being as truth, we expand and become more.

Who we are is continually changing, as is our experiential understanding of ourselves. As we change, we also change everything around us in ways we can't imagine – in part because who we are is so much more than we can ever imagine. Our resonance radiates throughout creation impacting everything everywhere.

Since we can't realize who we are with only our mind, how do we experience ourselves?

A new kind of language is needed:
a language of feeling,
of consciousness,
of experiencing,
of aliveness,
of *and..*

experiencing

We can become aware of experiencing in unexpected moments of expansion in which we feel exquisite love, beauty, or freedom.

When a baby smiles, emotions well up in us and our heart expands with love. Music moves us and our body reverberates with resonance. It's palpable and alive. It flows.

In those moments, with what or with whom are we connecting? We are experiencing the aspect of us that is always there underlying everything else. For a brief moment we touch it. We resonate with what's deeply within and around us, and we enter its flow. Suddenly we are seeing through different eyes that are at once softer yet clearer.

We tingle with waves of energy, warmth, substance, and light. We open into the world of resonance. It's that part of us that our eyes can't see and our ears can't hear, but that we can sense and recognize as our truest selves. It's indefinable and we experience it beyond our five senses. It vibrates and resonates.

When we identify only with our body or personality, we experience ourselves as finite. This is a world that can be measured and quantified. But when we feel the movement of our energy, substance, warmth, and light ever expanding, we are identifying with our infinite nature. This feeling is beyond ordinary emotion.

The air thickens, our thoughts slow down and we become aware of the space between our thoughts. In this space, we are able to distinguish between our thoughts, emotions and sensations. In this space we access a new and different connection with ourselves. In this space we taste something beyond our ordinary self as we open beyond our own limitations. In this space we enter the mystery. In this space we experience unspeakable intimacy as we resonate with all of existence.

This moving, pulsating aliveness is who we are. In fact, we are resonance itself. Our being resonates at different frequencies, and as we get to know them, we can choose from which to create in any given moment.

Through sensing our energy resonating we become aware that who we are is an expansiveness that is sentient, dynamic, interactive, and multi-dimensional. Who we are is extraordinarily and magnificently complex, yet simple and natural when experienced.

In being aware of our resonances, we touch our own consciousness, which is who we are. Consciousness is far beyond our current understanding of thoughts and feelings. While ineffable and intangible, we can experience it through our sensations, feelings, emotions and energy.

Resonance is the language of our consciousness.

It's an experience. While experiencing, we're connecting with our own consciousness. Our consciousness is aware of itself, and grows in that awareness the more we're present with it. In our ability to see ourselves with clarity, we are constantly transcending ourselves.

Consciousness can't be contained, explained, or put in a box. It can only be experienced for the joy of it.

Its resonance grows through its polarity, dissonance.

Imagine an upward spiral of evolution:
Dissonance → resonance
Resonance → dissonance
Dissonance → greater resonance
Resonance → further dissonance →
greater resonance

We tend to think of one as good and the other as bad. But, the deepening of consciousness as a consequence of embracing these polarities equally is a taste of *and...*

In this time in our collective awakening, we are ascending the spiral of evolution into the potential of an entirely new experience of ourselves as consciousness itself.

Through our expanded feeling senses
we experience our authentic selves.
As we awaken to this new sense of who we are
more deeply,
we become aware that we are consciousness,
whose presence
is in everything everywhere.

who we are

Who we are is not what we do. Rather, what we do is an expression of who we are.

Who we are is already there inherently, innately, and doesn't need to be proven; it's already so. When we become present with ourselves as an actual experience, we deeply know our true worth.

We are
an
ocean
of
sensations,
feelings,
emotions
and
thoughts,
constantly moving
and
changing.

We are a fluid, dynamic process
continually becoming.
We are a mystery
longing to be further explored.
We are an unlimited, continuous flow
of unfolding and enfolding complexity
beyond rational comprehension
but not beyond experience.

We are whole in who we are
even while
becoming
more.
We are lacking nothing.

We are far greater
than we can
possibly imagine.

In our limitlessness,
"I"
is much too small a word.
"We" is more embracing.

We are consciousness
exploring and discovering itself,
becoming more,
reverberating with resonance,
creating and expanding
infinitely.

enlightening

We have held an image of who we think we are and want to be. We've imagined that there's a place at which we will arrive one day and feel the way we want to feel forevermore. We call this place "Enlightenment."

But, there is no "There" to get to.
There's only Here.
Here is the present,
where we have access to our unlimited Self.

And there is no singular moment of
enlightenment,
Only ongoing enlightening.

Enlightenment means something to achieve.
Enlightening is a living process of discovery.
There is no finish line;
we go on forever.

When enlightening
we are
exploring,
discovering,
growing,
changing,
moving,
expanding,
flowing
and
becoming.

As we move beyond our current horizon,
it moves too
so we never reach the next horizon.
We are an endless event,
continuously expanding,
unfolding and enfolding
integrating and enlightening.
Everything is occurring simultaneously
including
death and rebirth.

Enlightening goes on forever.
And so do we.

integrating

Within our old operating system, we have a relatively limited experience of ourselves. Yet, we are made of many parts and are multi-dimensional. Within us are a child, an adolescent, a young adult, an adult, an ego, an infinite self, a finite self and so on. All parts have the same desire for love and hope but have different ways of trying to meet those needs. Each has its own point of view and feelings. All want to and can have their needs met.

Integrating our parts into an always expanding greater whole is the ongoing process of evolution. There is not a fixed place at which we arrive where we are finally fully integrated.

Integrating is not homogenization. Each part of us keeps its own unique and valuable identity while interrelating cooperatively within the greater whole. Like instruments in an orchestra, the individual parts harmonize to create a magnificent symphony.

There's nothing inherently bad about any of our parts or their feelings. While we outgrow acting upon the dictates of certain parts, we don't need to try to rid ourselves of these parts, including our shadow aspects and the masks we wear to conceal them. We're not broken and we don't need to be fixed.

There are some broken parts of us that never change, but it's not necessary that they do so. The more we try to fix and perfect ourselves, the more we suffer.

The way we regard these parts can change from rejection to acceptance, and from judgment to love.

It hurts when we blame, shame or exile any part of ourselves. We can hold enough tender space for all of our parts without needing them to change. Then they feel valued as part of the whole. We can wisely discern and make choices about which parts to follow by not rejecting and perfecting.

Every part of us is valuable, acceptable, and precious for what it is. It longs to be illuminated, not eliminated.

As we approach every part of us with understanding and compassion, enfolding it within our heart, the heart leads and the part follows. In this way, we are in harmony with all of our parts, as we conduct our inner orchestra and make the music that is our life.

Honoring, valuing and appreciating all of our parts for who they are and for what they contribute is part of integrating. When we appreciate our strengths and vulnerabilities for what they are, in that lovingly interdependent relationship, we create ourselves anew.

Every part of us
yearns to bask
in the light
of our tender regard.
Our heart is vast enough
to hold all.
We thrive in the rapture
of our love's
reverent embrace.

inner resources

When we feel the movement of our energy, substance, warmth, and light expanding, we are identifying with our infinite nature. In becoming present, we connect with our own vibrations, feelings
and resonances.

The more deeply we connect with
the one that we are,
the more we connect with Oneness.
The more deeply we connect in Oneness
with All-That-Is,
the more we know the one that we are.

This paradox is an experience of *and..*

In experiencing our connection with All-That-Is,
we have access to infinite resources of every kind,
since All contains all. All-That-Is lacks nothing,
and in our connectedness, neither do we.

Infinite resource
is
always there
waiting to be felt,
always accessible,
and
always becoming more.

When we don't feel these inner infinite resources and their resonances it's because we're not connecting with them; we believe that they are not part of us.

"I am *not* love itself," is the *knot*.
This *not* is the *knot* that binds and separates us from our inner resources.

Since these inner resources are who we are, not what we have or need to get, they are inviolate. When we feel our inner resonances, we can feel who we are inherently.

Within us, around us,
and who we are innately
is
limitless Love
overflowing abundance

inherent safety
unconditional belonging
absolute value
exquisite beauty,
sublime universal wisdom,
innocence and imagination
and so much more.

Since these resources are who we are, they are always there, but we're not always aware of them. It's the same with our connection with All-That-Is. It's always there, but as we grow in our awareness of that presence, our feeling of connectedness deepens. We expand through the ongoing process of connection to disconnection, of resonance to dissonance to a higher octave of resonance.

As we connect, we don't lose our individual self. To the contrary, the more we feel connected, the more we clearly experience our personal and universal resonances. The more we feel our resonances, the more deeply we know who we are and the more fully we enjoy ourselves.

all-that-is

Even though we are seemingly just one person, quantum physics has opened us to the understanding of our interconnectedness. Since we are one with All-That-Is, we are interconnected with all.

In our old paradigm, we identify ourselves as finite beings who occasionally touch the infinite. In the new octave of consciousness, we identify as infinite beings who express in the finite for the joy of it.

The infinite is more than big enough to hold the finite. In this expansive experience, we feel at one with ourselves and simultaneously with all that exists, or All-That-Is. This is another experience of *and..*

All is so much more than we now know or will ever know.
All-That-Is is not All That You Think That Is.
All-That-Is really is really *all* that is.
All, by definition, includes everything.
All includes us, as well as that which will forever be beyond our comprehension.

We are always growing, evolving,
and expanding;
so is All-That-Is.
Our nature is to expand and discover.
We can relish the richness
of what is right now
even while desiring more.

The more we're willing to feel our infinite nature, the more we expand and open. In so doing, we become more aware of our interconnectedness with All-That-Is. Our willingness to experience ourselves as one with All-That-Is allows for a deeper knowing of who we are.

As you know yourself as one with All-That-Is, you have access to all. Since you are part of All-That-Is, and so is everyone else, then everyone is part of you. As we recognize and accept each part of us, including our shadow, there is nothing to defend against or protect. We are all a part of everything everywhere.

Since we are finite and infinite,
universe and multi-verse,
we can paradoxically and simultaneously
experience
our individuality and connectedness
with All-That-Is.

feelings

How do we experience our connection with All-That-Is?

By feeling our feelings.
By welcoming our feelings.
By accepting our feelings.
By noticing when we are resisting feeling.
The key to feeling is just being willing to feel.

Which feelings?
All feelings.

What are feelings?

Authentic feelings are beyond what we usually think of as feelings. Real feelings have a palpable sensation of flow, vibration and scintillating light-filled aliveness. Feeling our realness or authenticity is experiencing the presence of our own resonance.

Why wouldn't we want to feel?
We're afraid of being hurt again.

We think that if we don't feel, we can stop the pain. So we try to not feel.

We avoid real feeling by pushing it away and retreating into our heads. We make up a story, or drama, which we believe is real. We become so involved in the story and its "emotions," we think we are feeling. But, the strategy has actually cleverly moved us away from our real feelings into thinking feelings but not actually feeling them.

When we do perceive a real feeling, we often move away from experiencing the feeling, while thinking we are feeling it. When we're thinking a feeling, it persists and we don't have a sense of release and relief into an expansion and an opening in which something resolves. Thinking feelings instead of actually feeling them recycles in a repetitive pattern. In recycling, we think the perception of a feeling is the same thing as feeling it. Instead of feeling, we engage in ideas about things, both positive and negative.

When truly feeling, we are connecting with the energy of an emotion. Then feelings move through us with relative ease and rapidity. The beautiful energy of real emotion moves, breathes, and is alive.

It's an entirely different sensation than what's produced by mental "emotions" or drama.

Feeling feelings is not terrifying. Even real intense grief, fear and dread feel good, as does excitement, when we let ourselves feel them. Fear is not bad and excitement is not good.

When are we not feeling?

When we contract, shut down, go stony cold, get hard, tense, and walled off. Then while not feeling, we perform emotion. Performed emotion is reactivity or "drama" masquerading as emotion. Drama, under the guise of feeling, is acting out. We habitually perform emotion instead of actually feeling it, all the while believing we are truly feeling. We misidentify drama as feeling, when we are actually thinking our feelings, not feeling them.

When we're dramatizing emotion, we're in our head. We're recycling a false belief that we lack something that we need, are separate from our source of fulfillment, and are powerless to get our needs met.

Then we "feel" a disempowered state of anxiety, outrage, despair, hopelessness, depression, hostility and vengeance. We sense that we are stuck, constricted, trapped, heavy, violent and dark. There's no flow or movement of life-giving energy through our body. This results in suffering.

Authentic feeling is natural and feels good. It's pure energy in motion, with no beliefs or stories attached. We have been very confused about what is authentic emotion. We take pains to avoid even real emotions because we have judged them as being negative.

Emotions like fear, anger, and sorrow are natural emotions far different than disempowered "emotions" of outrage, depression or anxiety. How do we recognize the difference between a disempowered state that we call a feeling, and real feelings?

Authentic feelings move. They're soft and feel good when we don't resist them. They flow easily, amplifying our resonance. All real feelings are rich with their own unique vibration, which is palpable, when we allow them to move through us as pure energy. Amazingly, they all feel good when felt and bring about release and relief.

Disempowered states feel bad because they result from not being willing to feel authentic emotion. They recycle. They are the resistance to feeling authentic emotions and don't feel good. For example, outrage, which we mistakenly call "rage," is actually a mask for powerlessness. When you allow yourself to feel powerlessness instead of fighting against it to try to become powerful, that brings relief. Then you can feel the bigger part of yourself right away.

Real feelings are neither good nor bad.
When we welcome our feelings, it feels good.
When we don't feel them, it feels bad.
When we suppress "bad" or painful feelings in order to feel good, it hurts.

If we judge and suppress emotions, we create tension. We become rigid with the effort it takes to not be overwhelmed by what we're trying not to feel.

If you were adrift in the ocean, desperately trying to prevent yourself from drowning, you would feel overwhelmed with tension. But, what if you realized that you are the ocean itself? You could revel in the exquisite pleasure of your own ever-changing currents, temperatures, and tides.

We are a flow of continuous movement. The flow of our energy is natural and effortless. It's tender and beautiful, rich and robust. When we restrict, reject or judge ourselves we block the flow, like a logjam in the river. Eventually, more and more energy concentrates around the logjam, which further reduces our natural flow. This cuts off our power.

Our deepest flow always flows. To the extent to which we are in alignment with it, we experience flow. The attempt to be perfect, or make ourselves other than who and how we are, shuts down our flow. In this way we stop some of the flow in ourselves, even though it never stops all around us. If we slow down, breathe, and move out of our mental stories and into our heart, we can feel again. We reconnect with the flow.

Every emotion, sensation and real feeling is valuable. There's no hierarchy of emotions. All are of equal importance when we actually feel them. When we reject our feelings, we don't value them as an integral part of our wholeness.

Change occurs through accepting and honoring the full range of our emotions and feelings. As we feel our authentic feelings, they open us into our inner resonance and connect us to our innate limitless resource.

Feeling the full range of our feelings
does not incapacitate us.
It empowers us,
impacts All-That-Is,
and
together
we become more.

impact

Our feelings impact all that exists every second of every day. Conversely, we are continually impacted by All-That-Is.

When we feel our feelings, their resonances naturally radiate out, having an effect upon all creation. Our true impact is far greater than we can comprehend.

The more we feel, the more impact we have. When we judge or reject our feelings, it stops the beautiful effect of our impact.

As I reveal more of my true feelings, I show you more of me. This allows you to be more of you, too. The more we reveal, the more richly complex, beautiful, and creative our experience.

When we keep our defenses in place, it diminishes our impact. As we retreat, withdraw, hide, or pull away, revealing less of who we are, we experience less, and have less impact. In withdrawal, we can be quite numb. This kind of separation from ourselves is extremely painful and greatly reduces our impact.

separating

Separation is a natural stage of development when we grow from infancy to adulthood.

First we are merged with the greater whole, with All-That-Is, but not yet truly individuated. This is like babies merged with their mothers.

Then, we perceive ourselves as separate to discover our unique identity. This is like children, adolescents and young adults carving out their own path and living their own lives.

Later, we discover that in addition to being an individual, we are also part of a greater whole. This is like young adults reintegrating into their original families but now interacting from their own strength.

That's a natural, healthy process. But there can be a kind of painful separation in which we feel disconnected. When we detach, retreat, become "objective" and resign in apathy we feel separated and it hurts.

These tendencies can come from our child part and can be healed by:

> Acknowledging the sense of separateness.
> Feeling the painful impact of it.
> Moving away from any self-blame and judgment
> Willingness to feel what's being denied
> Remorse about the pain it caused
> Compassionate self-forgiveness.
> Making a choice to connect.

The perspectives of our child part, while understandable in an early stage of development, may not work now. Through recognition and acceptance of the voices of our inner child's limited perspectives, we free ourselves from acting upon their advice or demands. Then, we become aware of the limitless perspectives that are productive in the present.

Our child's limited perspectives aren't bad; they're simply too small to contain all of who we are. When we tenderly include our more limited parts within the limitlessness of our greater whole, we experience harmony, integration and innovation.

Then we can choose to separate consciously, which is not painful. It's a joyous way to learn and grow. Its purpose is to get to know ourselves as distinct from a merged whole. It's a differentiation toward a higher level of integration.

Differentiation is like
a white light passing through a prism,
separating into a rainbow of colors.
The white light remains and
is revealed to contain a multiplicity of colors.

Once distinct,
the colors can play
with each other
in creative ways.
This is the fun of life
and how we grow.

When we choose to grow by
separating consciously,
we ascend the spiral of evolution,
simultaneously feeling
our

uniqueness
and
connectedness
with
All-That-Is.

This paradox is *and..*

connecting

Our desire to connect is the longing of our heart. We long to connect with more of who we are and with All.

The heart doesn't control or force. The heart feels. It calls, beckons and patiently invites. Our yearning to feel connected heeds that call, gently guiding us beyond separation.

Through the heart, we feel vastly expansive, inter-related, and connected to everything everywhere.

The more we connect,
the more alive we feel.
The more alive we are,
the more connected and whole we feel.

In feeling connected, we don't lose a sense of our individuated self. To the contrary, the more we feel connected, the more we experience our own resonances as the living truth of who we are. And, the more we experience our resonances, the more connected we feel.

Even though we are always inherently connected, we continue to grow in that experience. It's an ongoing process; it's not a goal that is finally achieved. Neither is it a merged state. We continue to experience who we are individually as we're connecting with All-That-Is.

Connecting is a continuous luminous expansion in unimaginable directions simultaneously like a star going supernova, in which you experience yourself as consciousness.

Connecting is a
a veritable romance with ourselves,
others,
and
All-That-Is.

As we are vibrating with the resonance of our infinite nature, we are uplifted beyond the painful sense of separation. In this new octave of consciousness we can live from our limitless inner resources, substance, light, and hope which give rise to a completely different outer reality than living from old stories.

As we begin connecting with these more expansive levels, we open multi-dimensionally. We know ourselves both as the person with whom we are currently identified, and also as more. In accepting our limited nature as well as our limitless resonances, we evolve.

When connecting through our heart, the movement of our consciousness in all directions is so expansive, it's far beyond our ability to comprehend. But it's not beyond our ability to experience. These precious moments of connectedness change our lives in ways we can't begin to imagine. But when we experience them we automatically trust them because they feel more real than anything else.

The more we feel connected, the more we are open to give and receive from All-That-Is. In the exquisite exchange within this experience of *and..* we powerfully amplify and impact each other.

happiness

There is no part of us, including our defenses, that is an obstacle to happiness. When we are aware of our defenses without judgment, we can choose when to keep them in place and when to let them down.

It's in thinking we need to be happy and positive all of the time that we create an obstacle to our happiness. It hurts when we push away from what we're actually feeling by trying to be happy.

Every part of us is a valuable part of the whole. When we welcome, accept and receive all of who we are with compassion, one feeling that arises is happiness. The more we come out into the light as our full selves, the happier we are, and the more we glow. As we can unwrap the presents and presence that we are by valuing ourselves and using our own gifts and talents, the happier we become. There's no right way to do that. All you have to do is show up as you. The more present we are, the happier we become.

Happiness flows from the acceptance
of who we are right now
and of
who we are becoming.

Our happiness has a positive impact.
It's a dynamic, co-creative part
of the great mystery of All-That-Is,
which delights in our presence.

The world and all that exists are conscious and interactive. This is an exciting leap in understanding the power of human consciousness. But that doesn't mean that we can now control the Universe. We can influence change by experiencing our happiness in dynamic exchange with All-That-Is. The currency of that exchange is gratitude.

Happiness, and its positive impact,
are like a beating heart;
they stir the flow,
unfolding into All-That-Is,
and enfolding from All-That-Is
back into us simultaneously.
In this movement we can feel
our true power.

true power

True power is an effortless flow within and around us, of such magnitude it is incomprehensible.

True power isn't control. Power through control is force. Force is hard, defended, tight, constricted, restricted and limited. It shuts down our feelings and flow. The more we don't feel, the more powerless we become, all the while desperately trying to gain power.

We render ourselves powerless by trying to become powerful through control and force. This is a formula for impotence.

The underlying beliefs are:

> I am separate.
> Life happens to me.
> I have no impact.
> I'm helpless.
> I'm weak and vulnerable.
> I must defend against vulnerability.

All feelings are threatening, therefore I must
   not feel.
I must do something to become powerful.
I must be in control.
I must never feel powerless.

When we recognize these beliefs are creating a
disempowered state, we stand at the doorway of
change. We step across the threshold by acknowl-
edging the pain and suffering that comes from
these beliefs.

Then we arrive at a choice:

   We can blame, shame, and punish ourselves,
      thus recycling the beliefs and
      perpetuating suffering, or...

   We can bring forgiveness and compassion to
      ourselves for entertaining these beliefs.

In the arms of compassion, we open into the gentle authentic feelings of our heart.

   There, we can see our stories for what they
      are.
   We can let go into the soft emotion of

powerlessness. Remember, authentic feelings are soft and move through us easily.

When we feel pure powerlessness with no story attached, it's a relief.
It relaxes the hardened clench of control and opens a doorway into the flow of true power.

In feeling the emotion of powerlessness, we surrender into real power.

Real powerlessness is an emotion we can feel; it's not the same as being powerless. Paradoxically, we are empowered by feeling the emotion of powerlessness. It's a huge relief to let go of control and let our true power emerge. But in the process of surrendering, our ego may resist giving up the illusion of control for fear that it is dying.

Being powerless disempowers us.
Feeling powerlessness empowers us.

It's a false assumption that we cannot get our needs met if we feel powerless. We can't get our needs met by being powerless. We do get our needs met by feeling the emotion of powerlessness. When we feel authentic emotion, its resonance is internally fulfilling. As we feel this power flowing through us, our external needs are effortlessly and creatively fulfilled.

Feeling the emotion of powerlessness opens us into the flow of true power.

Real power *includes* the feeling of powerlessness.

Powerlessness as a story = a disempowered state.
Powerlessness as an authentic emotion = a doorway into true power.
Embracing the paradox of feeling power and powerlessness = *and..*

In the resonance of *and..*
we embrace paradox and
become more of who we are,
while flowing with
limitless power
and
freedom.

freedom

Freedom is an unbridled feeling.
Freedom is when
you're floating in weightlessness
and can't fall because
there's no gravity anymore.

We can tell the difference between feeling trapped and feeling free. There's a relief that comes of freedom from imprisonment. If we go further, there's an ecstasy that comes from freedom into lightness and possibility.

There is freedom *from* and freedom *into*.

Both have to do with freedom, but we don't need to stop at freedom *from* restriction. The more profound change actually occurs with freedom *into* limitlessness.

Freedom *from* lifts us out of our old beliefs. Instead of staying stuck in what we've believed, we're now available to engage freedom *into*. It's a more luminous and expansive feeling of infinite possibility.

We feel limited when we're in the predicament of choosing one way or another, either/or. What if we don't need to choose between two things?

Freedom is in going beyond identifying with one possibility, thinking it's the *only* truth, for example, being right or being in control. When our concept of what's "right" is not the only truth, we open to a greater freedom. When we grow beyond the need to be right, we surprise ourselves with the joy, wonder and surprise inherent in freedom.

The paradigm of control is like a rechargeable battery that's losing its charge. Rather than trying to recharge the battery by looking for new strategies to maintain control, we can relinquish the imagined power of control. This is freedom *from*.

Freedom *from* is not a rejection or a pushing away. It's opening *into* more inclusivity. By bringing compassion to the part of us that wants to be in control, we include it as part of our wholeness.

Through inclusivity and compassion, we open further. In this dynamic fluidity, we revel in the thrill and vulnerability of risking openness *into* greater freedom and marvel at what emerges.

Sometimes we see things as only black or only white.
That's either/or.
When we see things as black and white and all shades of gray,
that's and/and.

Moving beyond either/or
is freedom *into*
something entirely new.
In this synergy of and/and
we experience ourselves as
a continually unfolding
complexity of flow.
In that flow
we feel ourselves
as an intrinsic part of All.

When we can include the part of us that doesn't accept who we are right now, *and* the part of us that does accept who we are right now, *and* the part that is opening into who we are becoming, then we are free.

This paradox of being present with these seemingly contradictory parts all at once is the process of *and..* from which new creation arises. This is freedom.

All that we truly wish to feel
exists in freedom.

Joy, compassion, innocence,
safety, confidence, wonder, value, belonging,
beauty, mystery, magic and creativity.

As we feel these ecstatic resonances
they rewrite our old programming
and
transform our reality.

In these suspended moments
of sublime freedom,
beyond space and time,
we realize that we create everything in
giving to and receiving from All.

receiving

Receiving is not a passive state.
It's a dynamic current
that offers engagement.
The more we open,
the more we receive
from All-That-Is.

All-That-Is has everything because it is everything.
It never stops giving. But we're not always open to
receiving. Sometimes, although we do receive, we
unwittingly throw away what has been given.

Based on past experience of not feeling safe, we
remain defended, often without being aware of it.
We continue to erect barriers for defense and protection. But barriers are impenetrable and don't
allow us to receive. They armor our heart and shut
down its flow.

Then we wonder why we're isolated, impover-
ished, unhappy, unhealthy, and unsuccessful. We
can feel alone in a crowd and not understand why.

We can have millions of dollars and never feel like it's enough.

Barriers are not boundaries.

Boundaries are like a cell wall, a permeable membrane. This allows the cell to maintain its distinct identity while receiving life-giving nutrients.

Boundaries are not barriers.

> With healthy boundaries
> we maintain a finite sense of self
> and
> simultaneously
> give to and receive from
> All-That-Is
> in luscious interconnectedness.

In limitlessness, we are inherently safe, without the need for walls of defense. There's nothing to protect against. The willingness to recognize our defenses, and bring understanding for having constructed them begins the gentle un-defending of our heart.

As we soften into feeling our inherent safety, we begin to receive. Receiving amplifies our flow, alters our reality, and uplifts us into realms of the miraculous.

The more we receive, the more we feel whole.
Then there's no black hole inside,
    compelling us back into control.
In control, we're erecting barriers of defense
    and not receiving.
Relinquishing control allows receiving
    through the tenderness of our heart.
In the resonance of receptivity, we open
    further into limitlessness and become
    available to receive more.

We don't need to earn receiving.
It's a natural function of being alive.
The idea of having to earn it
pushes it away.

More than we can imagine
wants to be given
as an unconditional gift.

We can unabashedly receive.

In the realms of the miraculous
we receive beyond our
wildest dreams and
ability to imagine.
In the depths of receiving
passionately
is great intimacy.

intimacy

True intimacy doesn't begin with another person. It's a deep and luscious communing with oneself and All-That-Is. When we experience ourselves as this Love, then being "in love" is not dependent on another person.

Real intimacy brings to light all that is not intimacy. In feeling the real Love within and around us, we feel fulfilled and met. Love's intensity increases as we touch it and are touched by it. The more we give and receive love, the more whole we feel. Then, the more able we are to give to and receive from others.

Within and around us is a wellspring of limitless Love from which we continually give and receive. This wellspring is who we are.

True intimacy is when we're in this Love, and simultaneously experiencing ourselves as this Love.

This feeling of *and..* is exquisite beyond delicious. It's a new sense of relating.

relating

Relating is an emotional experience that is continuously moving. It's not a static thing called "A Relationship." Relating happens when we have no agenda about outcome and instead remain present in the flow of each moment. Then something real and innovative emerges.

When we are in the current of our own intimacy and share it, relating occurs.

Relating is different than "trying to build a relationship." That's like two people trying to build a ship. Instead of authentically relating, trying to build a relationship can become a set of needs, demands, rules, contracts and expectations. In this case, the ship can sink.

When trying to build a relationship we are not present as our real selves. We tend to try to recreate what we think relationships should be based on an old model of fairytales, false hopes, and childhood dreams.

We look to a relationship to make us feel the way we want to feel. We try to change others – or ourselves – into who we want them to be or think we want to be. "If only this or that thing were different, then everything would be perfect. You would be 'The One.'" Or, we attempt to adapt to the expectations of others, and to be "The One" for that other person.

The two sides of the notion of "The One" can imprison and suffocate both people, who then wonder what happened to the beautiful flow they originally felt. We mistakenly try to restore the original feeling by trying to fix the form of the relationship. We try to fix each other and ourselves. Or conversely, we try to prove that we can meet all of our own needs by becoming overly independent.

When we impose a rigid structure of "relationship" on the flow of relating, it stops the flow. Then again the ship can sink.

When we impose the story of "The One" on the flow of relating, we deny that the source of Love is already within us. We look outside of ourselves to fill the hole.

However, "The One" can never fill the hole because there is no hole. It's a perception within a belief in lack. There is wholeness, however. The search for "The One" is fundamentally the longing to experience this oneness.

Instead of seeking "The One" and trying to build a relationship, we can choose to focus on relating. Then a beautiful dance occurs. The flow of relating creates the form of our relationships, which changes continually. Our relationships become more and more extraordinarily fulfilling, reflecting our own inner dance of intimacy.

Relating is where richness exists.

choice

When we have a full array of colors on a palette, we can choose the ones with which we want to paint. Likewise, when we have learned the keys on a piano, we are free to play the music we wish.

It's the same with knowing ourselves intimately. We can actually choose how we want to feel. Recognizing the difference between the ego's voice and the heart's desires is key to choice. True choice comes from our heart and is an emotional experience.

The ego likes to think it gets to choose. It focuses on what form it wants. It often believes, "I am limitless, I am powerful, I have a choice." Or, it can say, "I am powerless and have no choice." Both sides of this coin are actually the ego's attempt at control and manipulation.

When our ego realizes that it's not in control, it can become anxious and depressed. In those states of suffering, it may not seem like we have any other choice than to be stuck where we are. It seems that we are being victimized by something outside of us that is more powerful.

As we realize it won't work to try to choose through the ego, we can go to our heart and feel its luscious resonances. It contains all of our authentic feelings.

As we enter our heart and choose to feel, our frequency radiates out, creating a more optimal reality. Then change happens naturally from the choice to come from our heart.

Choice really means that we choose in which resonance we stand. When we are adept at this, we can choose which part of us drives the car. For example, we can choose to feel expansive lightness. Then through choice, we are not left hoping for, or waiting for a better feeling. Nothing more is needed when we are filled with all that we long to feel.

Every time we make the choice to feel our authentic feelings, whether joy or fear, the flow of these feelings rewrites our core programming. The simple awareness that we do have choice catalyzes change.

We change effortlessly by making the choice to feel connected with ourselves, others, and All-That-Is. In our sense of wholeness, we feel alive and grow through joy. Growing through joy is a choice. But, choice is not once and for all; it's again and again, little by little, and one choice at a time.

Authentic choice is one that expands our conscious awareness of our beautiful complexity and grace.

Choice changes everything.
Through choice, as our resonance is amplified, we are able to exercise even more power of choice…
…to choose the wonderful feelings in our heart…
…our heart's desires.

heart's desires

Heart's desires are feelings. They are not things to possess or goals to attain.

Like plucking a cello string, heart's desires vibrate; they resonate. They are resonances and emotional in nature because the heart feels.

Most people don't truly know their heart's desires. They think they do, but are unknowingly listening to their ego's demands. These demands masquerade as heart's desires, but they're not the same. "If I had this, then I would feel that."

We access our heart's desires through feeling. Feeling engenders a sweet vulnerability, which doesn't mean weakness. It means we are standing gently in our heart, undefended and open. This gives us authentic strength.

Being open is not a dangerous place to be, although it can often seem that way. In openness, we naturally have healthy boundaries so we don't need walls of protection. Open heartedness is not passivity or impotence. It's a vibrant, active state in which we experience ourselves as safe in our connectedness with All. Then there's nothing to protect or defend against.

Staying guarded and defended is painfully isolating. Armor is an energy block, a hardened, contracted state. It's a prison of loneliness in which we deny love even while yearning for it.

Yet, just declaring we are open does not let down the armor and open the heart. Opening begins by gently focusing within our heart and becoming non-judgmentally aware of the armor. As we meet our armor with gentle presence, it will express its resistance, then gradually soften.

As armor softens, it dissolves into rivers of tenderness. In these warm waves of energy, we feel loved, safe and at home.

When we are present in our own softness,
we can feel our heart's
true desires.

Even though we are taught that the mind reigns supreme, the mind is not large enough to encompass the heart. However, the heart's resonances are so vast and potent, they can embrace the mind. We can have faith in their beautiful, unpredictable flow. We can trust that our heart's desires are based not on our ego's demands, but on our true preferences and authentic needs.

When in our heart, we can consciously attune to what we most wish to feel, such as innocence, passion, hope and magic.

Heart's desires are
deep essential feelings.
Thus, feeling deeply in our heart
creates sublime reality.

As we identify with our heart's feelings there is no "work" to be done. The outer form of life unfolds gracefully from our heart's resonances.

Our heart burns with desire
to express.
Its stunning revelations
contain elements of delightful surprise.
Its rivers of resonance

inspire, animate, and create
our finite world,
effortlessly precipitating
into form.

form

The outer form of our lives comes from the resonances of our consciousness. Our resonances effortlessly create form. As the vibratory frequency of our consciousness increases, life becomes correspondingly playful and magnificent.

> Outer form arises from inner resonance.
> Our life is an expression of this resonance.

But that's not what we believe. We think that our thoughts and feelings are caused by outer circumstances. Consequently, we believe we have to manipulate external conditions to attain the results we think we want. This programming is so strong that we generally don't even notice or question it.

Our old programming is like the software in a computer. You don't get any answers other than those generated from that program. The program doesn't think or feel. It's limited in its functionality to whatever it was designed to do. It follows its own rules and limitations.

This old programming has a limited repertoire to fix, judge, punish, perfect and control in order to "survive." It has us convinced that our survival is at stake. The program generates thoughts and feelings to validate its point of view.

But most of what we call thinking and feeling is actually part of the programming—rigid lines of code that we believe are authentic. They fabricate the story we call "reality." As long as we're within this program, the form that emerges is not innovatively creative.

The vast expanse of true thinking and feeling exists far beyond our programming. It's beyond what we know and beyond what we know that we don't know. It's in the territory of what we don't know that we don't know. This is a profoundly fertile place for transformation and new form.

True thinking is not native to any idiom. It has no built-in story, history, future projection, or interpretation attached. True thinking and feeling are spontaneous revelations of our ever-expanding consciousness, which is infinitely creative.

Innovation arises from the enthralling beauty of this aliveness. The more present we are, the more effortlessly our lives unfold into form as a wondrous expression of the radiance of our resonances. In this endless expansion of our being are unimaginable grandeur, magic, pleasure and grace.

The form that we create called "life" is only the smallest expression of our creativity. We ourselves are actually our most magnificent creation. When we mistakenly value form above all else, we're in a limited loop recycling old programs. But when we value who we are, we create form spontaneously as a gorgeous expression of the resonances of our heart.

response-ability

Response-ability is spontaneously creating our heart's true desires, which are emotional in nature and are resonances. Instead of reacting from limited possibilities, we are responding from our limitless inner resource. This is response-ability, and all of us have this ability to respond.

Responsibility has commonly meant, "I am responsible. It's all up to me. I must be in control and make it happen. Or, I must get someone to give it to me." When that doesn't occur, we can become anxious and even panicky.

This old definition of responsibility is really reactivity, which denies us access to the infinite inner resource of our resonances. Trying to create from reactivity is like trying to navigate impossibility instead of creating from limitless possibility. The old version of responsibility offers the promise of possibilities, but never delivers the goods. Its potential solutions can even be punishing. To live by its suggested strategies is a kind of cruelty to ourselves, which drains, rather than fills us up.

Control doesn't create from our heart's desires. But, we can choose to respond from our limitlessness resonances instead of reacting from limited possibilities. In this responsiveness, we are creating from our heart's desires.

creating

Creating is a process that occurs spontaneously beyond our understanding and beyond time and space. It's so natural, that we're not aware of our consciousness creating in each moment in concert with All.

Persistent feelings of powerlessness not withstanding, we actually create ourselves, and our entire universe out of the great mystery. We are not created by the mystery as if it were something separate or outside of who we are. We are part of All, creating ourselves. We are either doing that consciously or unconsciously, but in either case, we are creating.

Each of us is a limitless and powerful creator. What if we could be aware of creating while creating? What if we could consciously co-create our heart's desires in partnership with All-That-Is? That creative collaboration is the true joy and potential of being human.

When we don't do this, we think reality is fixed and life just happens to us. We believe we have to work hard to make life work. This context of necessary hard work is the common understanding of creating, but this obscures the truth.

When we don't truly recognize how creation works, which is that form arises as a spontaneous expression of our consciousness, we revere and cling to the known old form we have already created. Then, we also believe we didn't create it. We become very attached to form itself, as if it's the only reality. We idolize the form that we create over the process of creating.

We're taught that we create by being in control. But contrary to popular belief, this method empties us out instead of filling us up, drains us instead of fulfilling us. When we connect to our true being, it guides and animates our doing. Then we create playfully and effortlessly.

Creating is not the same as producing something. That is productivity. Productivity flows out of our creativity naturally when we are connecting with the flow of our consciousness.

We long for new experiences and fresh ideas. We long to feel inspired and surprised. We yearn to feel our power expressing from our limitless nature, beyond the ordinary.

As we move into a new octave of consciousness, we become aware of the energy that is creation itself. When we feel ourselves at one with this energy, we can experience ourselves as part of creation creating. As we are conscious of creating while creating, we can also become aware that we are co-creating.

This awareness amplifies our power to create and represents a quantum leap forward in creativity. The old version of creativity is productivity intended for survival. The new version is creating simply for the joy of it.

When creativity inspires productivity out of pure joy, then what we produce re-inspires our creativity. When we create from gratitude, wonder and beauty, our impact is evolutionary.

Our new world will emerge from the infinite possibilities of what is not yet known. New creation emerges from the Unknown.

unknown

The Unknown is a live being. It's sentient. It's not absent or devoid of something. The power of the Unknown is that it holds all possibilities. Innovation comes out of the Unknown.

Exploring the unknowable is really exploring new parts of who we are. When we touch the intangible, it touches us.

However, we tend to avoid what is unknown, fearing that impenetrable darkness, danger or even death lurk there. We turn away or try to understand it in order to feel safe. We always want to know ahead of time, instead of discover over time.

If we could understand the Unknown, it wouldn't be unknown and All wouldn't be infinite.

Instead of trying to know the Unknown beforehand, why not get to know it? Trying to know is control, while getting to know is discovery.

Discovery is different than striving to find out, or thinking we already know.

> When we think we need to know,
> we tighten and contract.
> When we discover,
> we open up
> and expand.

We can't control what's unknown, but we can relate to it with curiosity, openness, and appreciation. Through discovery, what was unknown becomes revealed; possibility becomes probability, then actuality. And there's always more unknown.

In any moment, we can be willing to let go of everything we've known. Whether inspired to do so or "forced" through crisis, we can become interested in something more.

As we open, we can't force ourselves to let go of what we currently know. But we can gently slip below the surface of what we've known. Despite our fears, we won't drown or lose ourselves. We will actually find more.

I'm willing to learn about myself beyond
    who I think I am.
I'm willing to go beyond what I think I want.
I'm willing to entertain that reality is more
    than I currently imagine, or can
    ever imagine.
I'm willing to be open to ongoing discovery.

Discovery
is
our soul's call
to adventure.

As we enter into an adventurous relationship with the Unknown, it becomes less scary. It becomes an intimate companion that is responsive and that delights in the connection. You can feel its joy in communicating. We can safely and happily surrender into its embrace. We change as a result of this relationship, and so does the Unknown. We become partners in a powerful and thrilling co-creation.

As we surrender into this relationship,
we become
light, powerful and free.
Change happens spontaneously as
what was previously unknown becomes known.

Fear of the Unknown
is fear of change.
But in relating to the Unknown
life is a beautiful and rewarding dance
with uncertainty and healthy chaos.

chaos

Chaos is alive, dynamic energy that exists within and all around us as a powerful force of creation. It is unpredictable movement within the Unknown, which contributes to innovation, creativity and change.

We think of chaos as dangerous, unruly disorder to avoid. But within its mysterious movement is an implicit order of elegance we cannot immediately perceive, but that contains all possibility. Its unexpected nature helps us grow and change.

Within chaos is an implicit order.
Chaos without order deteriorates into anarchy.
Within order is the beautiful unpredictability of chaos.
Order without chaos becomes tyranny.
Their synergy births stunning creativity.

Chaos doesn't bend to our will. We can't contain it, control it or comprehend it any more than we can know the Unknown prior to discovering some

aspect of it. But when we allow ourselves to part-
ner with its dynamic energies and implicit order,
it's not destructive. It expands us beyond comprehension and even beyond imagination.

Our interaction with chaos brings new revelations,
creativity and change. It precedes and follows
change. We can choose to enter chaos to explore
new directions and grow.

Chaos is a gift that lifts us to a higher resonance.
From this more expansive perspective, we can see
the limitations of our old beliefs. Chaos is not logical, nor reasonable. It pulls, calls and stretches us.

When we surrender into the pure energy of chaos,
we discover the quiet center within it. As we dwell
in the silence and stillness within unpredictable
movement, we become aware of wondrous possibilities. Chaos becomes a joyous experience full of
power and creativity, liberating us into spectacular
new realities.

As we welcome and befriend chaos,
valuing it for what it is,
it changes us.

Our limitless nature
includes
chaos
and
change.

change

Change is exciting but can elicit fear and dread. Right now, the magnitude of change in our world is so great it's almost incomprehensible.

We have always been changing, but only in small, sometimes imperceptible increments in ages past. The depth and speed of innovation at this time is a quantum leap into something entirely new and different. In the perpetual, exponential movement of change, it's understandable that this can arouse fear.

Change is the nature of being. It happens every second of every day. Yet, even when we love evolving, it can be extremely challenging.

What's threatening about change
is that we actually change!

We don't change and then get back to normal. In change, there is no normal.

The part of us that wants normalcy is hardwired to resist change. This resistance is the fear of going beyond what we currently know.

Resistance to change is normal. We can stay entrenched in a painful and often damaging cycle of resisting the inevitable. To stop things from changing, we try to preserve form. But then, like putting a rose in acrylic, we can't feel it, touch it, smell it, or witness its beautiful unfolding.

When we believe that change is terrifying, we try to be in control to avoid imagined loss, pain, danger or death. This engages our survival strategies. In our fight or flight mechanism, we think feeling renders us vulnerable. So we refuse to feel, thinking that this will make us stronger and more resilient.

> When we avoid feeling,
> we avoid change.
> To avoid change,
> we avoid feeling.

We are terrorized by our ideas about change, not by change itself.

Beyond our ideas about change, the powerful energies of evolution are always moving. When we fight against them, crisis occurs. That's one way to change.

A more gentle approach is to meet, experience, and move through our resistance. As we tenderly embrace the parts of us that feel threatened, we are able to feel their underlying dread, sadness, anger, excitement and hope. As we feel our emotions, we change.

Authentic emotion carries us into wondrous freedom when we experience its pure energy without a story attached. Therefore, feeling our dread and fear along with our excitement allows change to change us.

When we feel, we change.
Feeling changes us.

Change itself is always happening, but we only shift when we align with it. Then we can ride the momentum of change. It doesn't work to simply think about, or want to shift. Letting go of our hardwiring requires choice and authentic emotional experience, not just intellectual understanding.

We change a little at a time, and not by force of will. But, we can become willing to surrender into it. Innovation can change everything, even our hardwiring, but it truly requires letting go of everything. When we invite it, welcome it, and actively participate in it, we change gracefully.

Change is an ally and friend.
We are always changing.
In fact, we are change itself.

We can appreciate, celebrate, and even seek out change.
We can delight in change truly changing us.

Change begins with us.
To change the world, we change ourselves.
Nothing changes until we do.
Everything changes as we do.
By changing ourselves,
we become creators of a new reality
through the discovery of new truth.

truth

Truth is something we feel deeply within. We experience it emerging as revelation. Through feeling, our flashes of insight become embodied and known to us. Deep knowing is not cerebral; it's a synergy of fresh thinking and feeling. Living truth is always novel.

New truth doesn't come from old paradigm thinking. When we hold onto what we already know, we block new truth from revealing itself. Everything we think we know exists within a closed loop. Every belief, attitude, choice, decision, thought and feeling within the old system is limited. Yet, we believe it is "the" truth.

What we currently agree upon as truth is certainly not all that exists. It may not even be accurate, even though we all agree about it, and it feels "right" to us. Agreement is different than truth; it's a collective mental construct. It's the best we've known at any stage of development, but it doesn't continually transcend itself like truth does.

This old version of truth exists within parameters that never evolve, which is contrary to the real nature of truth. When we hold onto what we already believe, we forego experiencing, through which we discover greater truths.

Since we have access to limitless knowing, when we are willing to expand beyond what we already know, we are open to experiencing deeper truths. We can receive from true knowing rather than filling in the blanks with what we think we know. We can ask questions without requiring answers. Truth is discovered beyond explanations, interpretations, and conclusions.

Since reality is comprised of infinite possibilities, and so are we, there isn't a singular or ultimate truth about anything. Truth is relative, depending on who is doing the observing. It is also relative to which part of us is doing the observing. If we perceive ourselves through a finite part, we will draw limited conclusions. As soon as we label those as "The One" truth or right/wrong, we're trapped.

Our perceptions of ourselves are miniscule compared to the immensity of who we actually are. Each new truth exists beyond our current interpretation of ourselves, and gives rise to an entirely new reality. Truth animates, imbues, and guides action in new directions.

Truth is a continual discovery, and all truth is not already known, nor will it ever be. What we know for certain is that truth is beyond our intellectual knowing. But, we are hardwired to be uncomfortable with not knowing, so we keep referencing from what we already know.

The willingness to not know opens us up to discover more. When we're unwilling to be with the discomfort of the unknown, we make up stories to try to fill that space. Since these stories exist within old paradigm thought, when we're there, we're not open to revelation.

If we sit in the discomfort of not knowing, and connect with the resonant field of the Unknown, revelation can emerge. What we need to know will be there when we need to know it, and not a moment before.

Welcoming
the incomprehensible Unknown
as the mystery that it is

allows quantum leaps
in truth.

Truth
animates new life.

life

We tend to think of life as a hand of cards we're dealt. Then, it's up to us to make the best of it. But what if life is not random, accidental or arbitrary? What if life doesn't just happen to us?

Through the events of life we discover more about who we are. Like looking in the mirror, we get to know ourselves. We learn through the experience of being finite, which is learning through limitation. Since we can't do everything we want to do, limitation gifts us with the chance to distinguish between what we do and who we inherently are. Then we can discover and choose what we truly want from our heart.

Limitation is like a magnifying glass or high-resolution microscope. It amplifies our beliefs to such a high level of clarity that we can become more aware of what they are. Through this discernment we can make more productive choices, and evolve through exercising the power of choice.

Everything in life is generated from our consciousness. The frequencies of our consciousness emanate like a broadcast. We are made of constantly moving waves of frequency that interact with other wave frequencies. Their interaction is dynamic and magnificently complex. The more complex (not complicated), the more creative and alive we become.

This constantly moving complexity of waves precipitates into form, creating life. Their interaction also creates the optical illusion of a wave that is standing still. We perceive this standing wave as matter. But matter isn't solid. These waves continually interrelate with each other in a way that is mutable, not fixed.

In this dynamism, our consciousness expands. It's the delight of consciousness to know itself more. As it becomes increasingly aware of itself, it evolves. Life gifts us with more and more of that experiential knowledge of ourselves.

We create life from our consciousness as a way to learn, but it happens mostly without our awareness that we are creating it. Yet, all of our experiences, the beautiful and the difficult, are our creation.

Our life is like a map of our beliefs, thoughts and emotions. It's an accurate reflection. When we don't have conscious awareness of our own beliefs, we think events are happening to us. The events help us get in touch with what is going on inside. Each event is like the next scene in the play of life – it's one long conversation with threads running through it. When we inquire into what we've created rather than blaming and judging ourselves, insight about these threads can occur.

Our particular path is no accident.
We're not an accident.
Our life is not a mistake.
We're not a mistake.

Your life is for you, and living your life is for you. It's an expression of the flow of your own consciousness. Our consciousness is the substance of life itself and generates everything. It's who we are.

But we can't control our consciousness. That would be like trying to stop the ocean's waves with our hand. The finite can't control or contain what's infinite. Our consciousness has its own currents, tides and natural flow. The flow flows.

The more we try to control the flow, the more painful and tragic the results. But as we un-defend and surrender into it, we realize there's nothing to defend against. The flow is not just out there somewhere, it's within us and it's who we are.

When we know ourselves as the flow itself, there is no outside authority to reward or punish us. There is only our own authorship. We are each not only the author, but also the director and all of the actors in our own play. Since life is our own creation, we can trust it. While we can't trust the content of the crazy stories our negative ego makes up, we can trust the flow of our consciousness that's more expansive than the negative ego.

When connected to that flow, we get to know ourselves and there's nothing to protect against. Thus, the concept of protection becomes invalid. The more we discover about ourselves through the process of life, the more our consciousness expands. But life isn't just about what we learn; it's about the joy of the process of living and learning itself.

As we are present with the process,
each moment becomes a joyful discovery.

Life becomes magnificent, even when challenging, a gift of great love we give ourselves to grow.

The fun of life is the exploration and discovery, revelation and creation. It's an ongoing experience, not a performance. The experience is in the feeling. It's an exploration, not an explanation.

Luckily, life will never be perfect. Perfection implies that it's finished, but life doesn't end. It's always shifting and changing. It moves and breathes, unlike perfection, which is static.

The point of life isn't to tolerate it, endure it, get through it, or get it over with. We can revel in, celebrate, and delight in its wondrous complexity. That includes feeling our resistance to aliveness. When we're resisting, we anxiously ask what we're supposed to be doing and who we're supposed to be. We endlessly demand that we be other than who we are and that life be different than it is. In so doing, we miss the magic and throw away possibility.

When we superimpose our agenda upon life seeking outcome and reward, we miss the richness of life itself. We second-guess ourselves, and want to know everything in advance. We ascribe meaning and interpretation, both positive and negative, to everything and everyone.

Instead, when we accept life as our creation, including our resistance as part of the process of life, we can learn from what we resist. When we don't judge resistance as wrong, we can welcome it, embrace it and move through it. Then the journey of life becomes magnificent, and resistance is just resistance; it doesn't mean anything about who we are inherently.

We came to Earth by choice to grow in further aliveness. In so doing, we open into ever-increasing intimacy with ourselves and All-That-Is. Life can be an entertaining way to learn, like a game that's stimulating, challenging and rewarding.

Who we are stretches far beyond any one lifetime. Since infinity is indeed infinite, it couldn't possibly be squeezed into one lifetime. Any single lifetime is like an individual rose in a garden full of roses. A single rose can't perceive or comprehend that it's in a garden of other roses, or other lifetimes, which are present simultaneously. From the perspective of the one rose, it may not know that it's part of oneness. Yet it is.

Life is like a short dream.
When our life story
seems almost insignificant,
we wake up within the dream,
vibrating with consciousness,
rich with aliveness.

When we physically die,
it's also like waking up from the dream
because consciousness is eternal.

Life is about experiencing our finite nature and our limitlessness. We can appreciate each for what it is, without trying to force one to be the other. Then we can live as an integrated whole, finite and infinite simultaneously.

There is such beauty and fragility,
joy and sorrow in being human.
By embracing these complexities,
we can consciously create life by choice.

When we welcome life as it is, we can see the aliveness in all things. Everything doesn't have the same consciousness, but everything has aliveness. Life itself is alive. It's a great gift and within its depths is magic.

The nature of magic is not linear or logical, and it doesn't follow our ideas about how it should be. When operating at its highest levels, it leaves no evidence of its presence. Thus, life can change instantaneously, as if "by magic."

In the complexity

of this aliveness

we create

from

the consciousness

born of

the

paradox

of

and..

the paradox of *and...*

And so we arrive at the paradox of *and...*

Paradox is an inextricable part of the new octave of consciousness, but not something the linear mind can comprehend. The mind thinks in either/or:

Infinite/finite
harmony/disharmony
connectedness/separateness
chaos/order
good/bad
solitude/loneliness
acceptance/anticipation
fear/excitement
human/divine
I/All-That-Is

Either/or is not complex enough to encompass paradox. By insisting on either/or, we reject or ignore contradiction, causing constriction.

However, when we feel more than one thing at the same time, embracing polarities and contradiction, we expand. What's exciting is that in the grand sweep of our human development, we've arrived at the possibility of embracing paradox.

First, we experience ourselves as undifferentiated, merged with All-That-Is. Then, we differentiate in order to discover our unique identity. Without losing our unique identity, keeping our differentiation, we discover a new kind of interdependent complexity by consciously reintegrating with All-That-Is. In this partnership, we and All-That-Is evolve.

In this stage of development, we experience our individuality and union, our differentiation and integration at the same time. An integrated person is aware of their darkness and light, their love and hate, and has come to a deep acceptance of all parts. As such, the individual components cooperate and work as a unified whole.

As we
become aware of
and deeply accept
all of who we already are

we become aware that we are
also becoming more
at the same time.

That's the paradox of *and..*

Within this inclusivity are extraordinary paradoxes, interconnectedness and co-creativity. They give rise to re-enchantment, expansive consciousness and new creation.

and.. births new creation.
and.. is evolution.

Who we are becoming is so extraordinarily different, it can feel as if we're being reborn in the same body. Remember, a butterfly is not a caterpillar with wings. We're transcending who we were. This uncharted territory is an extraordinary adventure in which we are learning to fly.

Is this enlightenment? No. There isn't a place or achievement called enlightenment. There is continuous integrating and enlightening, unfolding and becoming. We never arrive and it never stops.

As we come to know more of who we are, at the same time we know more of All-That-Is. As we simultaneously embrace who we are uniquely, our union with All-That-Is, and who we and All-That-Is are becoming together, we experience *and..*

Our exquisite uniqueness
in concert with All-That-Is
is a mutually thrilling love affair
in which we all rejoice.

A romance,
intensely alive,
utterly sensual,
sublimely erotic,
passionate and fulfilling.

A dance of
enthralling pleasure,
luscious communing,
inexpressibly joyous entwining.

Never ending,
eternally deeper, broader, richer,
more expansive
luminous,

intense,

intimate.

Exquisite

beyond delicious,

and..

All-That-Is yearns to engage with us just as we yearn to experience All. All-That-Is invites us to come play and create as companions. In the magnificence of this partnership, we delight in ourselves, each other, and All-That-Is.

As we surrender further into this sublime intimacy, we are not forsaking our finite self. Surrender is not a giving up of oneself. To the contrary, we get to know ourselves more intimately.

In this intimacy, as we experience the majesty of our own dignity, character, authority, and freedom, we can consciously integrate with All-That-Is. We integrate not with what we think or imagine All is, but what it truly is. As we consciously walk with All-That-Is, we can authentically co-create, creatively impacting each other.

In the depths of this magnificence, we experience a higher octave of Love in which we are one with Creation consciously creating itself. *and...* is a fusion reactor of creation. It's like the sun opening up inside of us full of substance and light, moving in all directions simultaneously. This is the true meaning of enlightening. As such, we birth, rather than control reality, and we all become more. This is true artistry.

Real artists don't know ahead of time what they're creating. They stand with delight in the convergence of the unfolding and enfolding of All-That-Is. The confluence of All-That-Is converging as a singular point of space, time and consciousness miraculously creates the matter that is you. This is your personal "big bang."

I am me
and
one with All-That-Is,
continuously integrating and enlightening,
and
becoming more of
who I am,
and
more of

who we are
and..

Each exquisite moment of *and..* changes our
lives forever.
We become an artist of life itself,
birthing creation.

And, more important than *who* or *what* we're becoming
is *that* we're becoming.

Printed in Great Britain
by Amazon